Can You See It?

D1180977

by **Jay Dale**

illustrated by Natalie Ball

Where is the green frog?
Can you see it?

It is hiding in the tree.
It looks like a leaf.

The snake will **not** see the green frog.

Where is the red fish?
Can you see it?

It is hiding in the coral.
It looks like the coral.

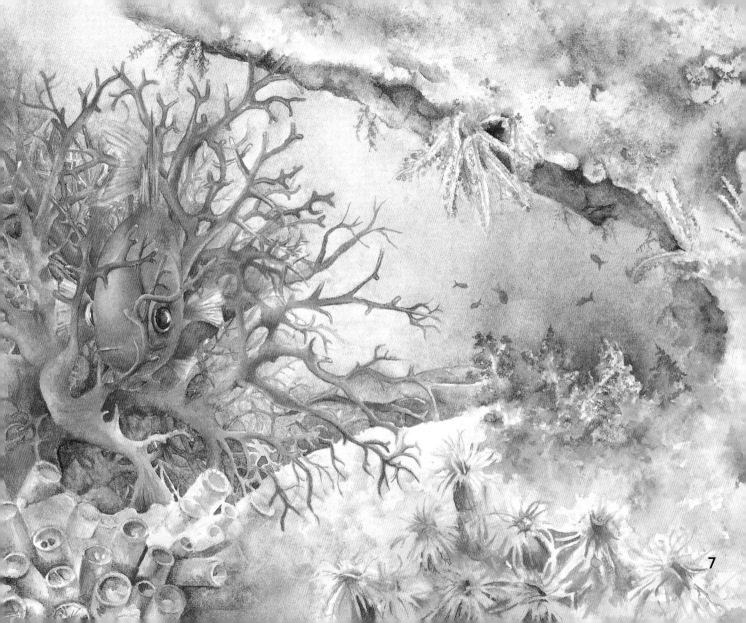

The shark will **not** see the red fish.

9

Where is the brown lizard?
Can you see it?

It is hiding in the sticks.
It looks like a stick.

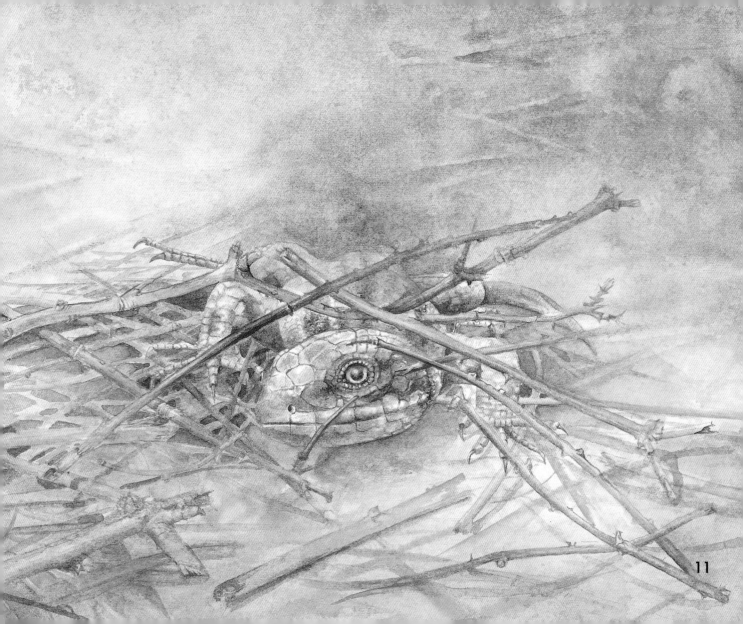

The snake will **not** see the brown lizard.

13

Where is the fox?
Can you see it?

It is hiding in the snow.
It looks like the snow.

The bear will **not** see the fox.